PIANO • VOCAL • GUITAR

GOOD OL' COUNTRY

ISBN 0-634-00735-1

HAL•LEONARD®
CORPORATION

7777 W. BLUEMOUND RD. P.O. BOX 13819 MILWAUKEE, WI 53213

Visit Hal Leonard Online at
www.halleonard.com

CONTENTS

ABILENE

Words and Music by LESTER BROWN,
JOHN D. LOUDERMILK and BOB GIBSON

AUCTIONEER

Words and Music by LEROY VAN DYKE
and BUDDY BLACK

(Spoken:) Hey, well all right, Sir, here we go there, and what're ya gonna give for 'em. I'm bid twenty-five, will ya gimme thirty, make it thirty, bid it to buy 'em at thirty dollars on 'er, will ya gimme thirty, now five, who woulda bid it at five, make it five, five bid and now forty dollars on 'er to buy 'em there...

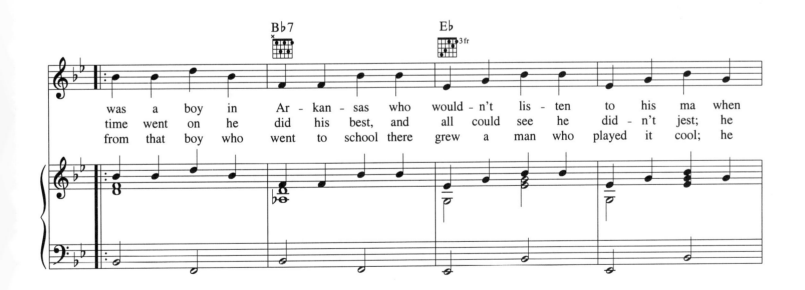

was a boy in Ar-kan-sas who would-n't lis-ten to his ma when
time went on he did his best, and all could see he did-n't jest; he
from that boy who went to school there grew a man who played it cool; he

8

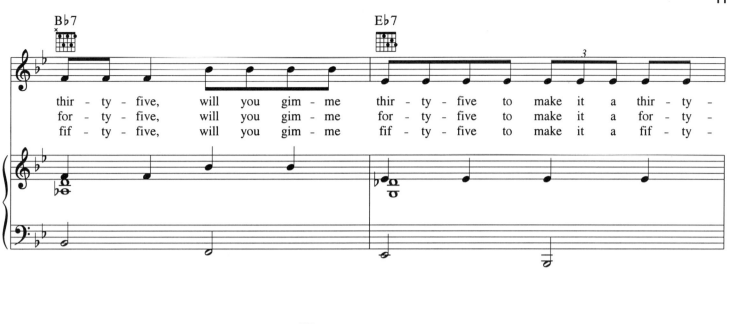

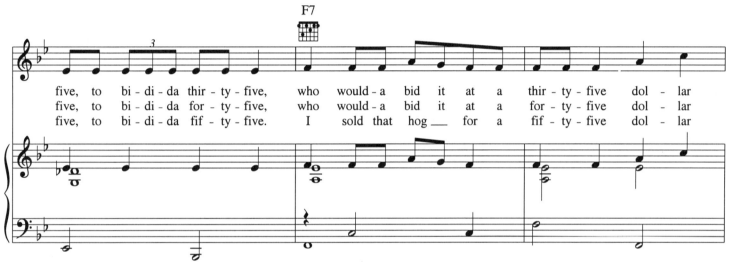

(Spoken:) Hey, well all right, Sir, open the gate an' let 'em out and walk 'em, boys! Here we come with lot number 29 in, what'd ya gonna give for 'em? I'm bid twenty-five, will ya gimme thirty, make it thirty, bid it to buy 'em at thirty dollars on 'er, will you gimme thirty dollars on 'er, now five, thirty-five, an' now the forty dollars on 'er, will you gimme forty, make it forty, now five, forty-five an' now the fifty dollars on 'er, will you gimme fifty, now five, fifty-five, an' now the sixty dollars on 'er, will you gimme sixty, make it sixty, now five, who'd-a bid it at sixty dollars on 'er to buy 'em there...

ANY TIME

Words and Music by
HERBERT HAPPY LAWSON

BIG BAD JOHN

Words and Music by
JIMMY DEAN

Verse 1. Every morning at the mine you could see him arrive,
He stood six-foot-six and weighed two-forty-five.
Kind of broad at the shoulder and narrow at the hip,
And everybody knew you didn't give no lip to Big John!
(Refrain)

Verse 2. Nobody seemed to know where John called home,
He just drifted into town and stayed all alone.
He didn't say much, a-kinda quiet and shy,
And if you spoke at all, you just said, "Hi" to Big John!
Somebody said he came from New Orleans,
Where he got in a fight over a Cajun queen.
And a crashing blow from a huge right hand
Sent a Louisiana fellow to the promised land. Big John!
(Refrain)

Verse 3. Then came the day at the bottom of the mine
When a timber cracked and the men started crying.
Miners were praying and hearts beat fast,
And everybody thought that they'd breathed their last 'cept John.
Through the dust and the smoke of this man-made hell
Walked a giant of a man that the miners knew well.
Grabbed a sagging timber and gave out with a groan,
And, like a giant oak tree, just stood there alone. Big John!
(Refrain)

Verse 4. And with all of his strength, he gave a mighty shove;
Then a miner yelled out, "There's a light up above!"
And twenty men scrambled from a would-be grave,
And now there's only one left down there to save; Big John!
With jacks and timbers they started back down
Then came that rumble way down in the ground,
And smoke and gas belched out of that mine,
Everybody knew it was the end of the line for Big John!
(Refrain)

Verse 5. Now they never re-opened that worthless pit,
They just placed a marble stand in front of it;
These few words are written on that stand:
"At the bottom of this mine lies a big, big man; Big John!"
(Refrain)

BLUE EYES CRYING IN THE RAIN

Words and Music by
FRED ROSE

BONAPARTE'S RETREAT

Words and Music by REDD STEWART
and PEE WEE KING

Brightly

Met the

girl I love in a town 'way down in Dix - ie 'Neath the

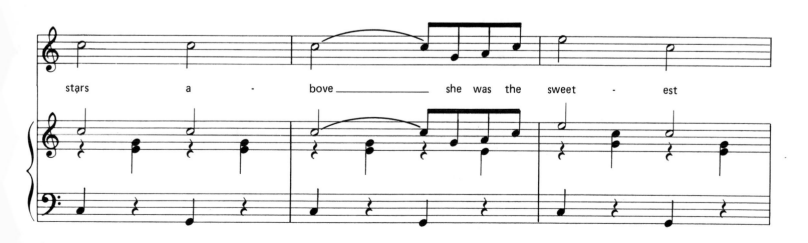

stars a - bove ____ she was the sweet - est

BORN TO LOSE

Words and Music by
TED DAFFAN

CANDY KISSES

Words and Music by
GEORGE MORGAN

BOUQUET OF ROSES

Words and Music by STEVE NELSON
and BOB HILLIARD

COLD, COLD HEART

Words and Music by
HANK WILLIAMS

32

CRAZY

Words and Music by
WILLIE NELSON

Lyrics (vocal line):

Cra - zy, _____ cra - zy for feel - in' so

lone - ly; _____ I'm cra - zy, _____

CRAZY ARMS

Words and Music by RALPH MOONEY
and CHARLES SEALS

CRYIN' TIME

Words and Music by
BUCK OWENS

CRYING IN THE CHAPEL

Words and Music by
ARTIE GLENN

Slowly, with expression

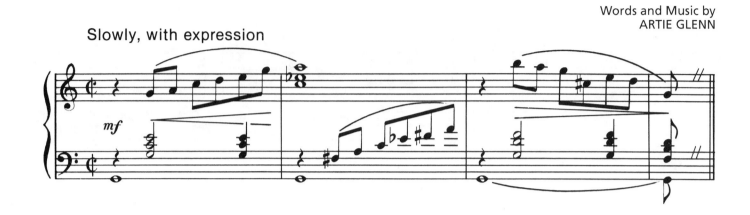

Chorus

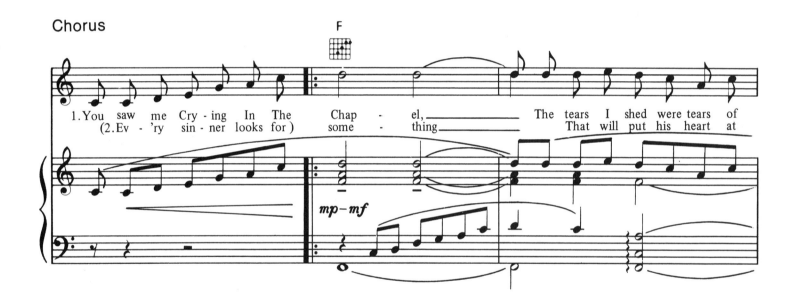

1. You saw me Cry-ing In The Chap-el,_____ The tears I shed were tears of
(2. Ev-'ry sin-ner looks for) some-thing_____ That will put his heart at

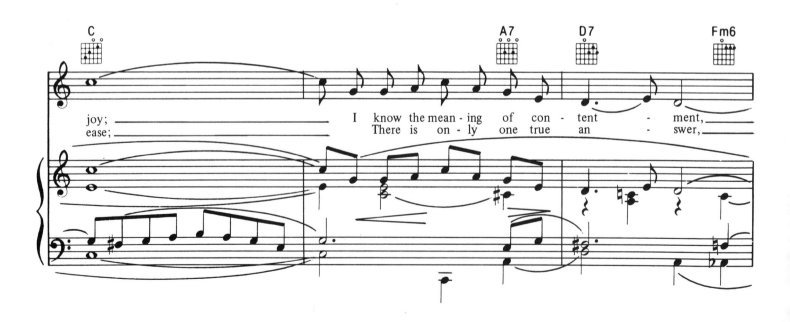

joy;_____ I know the mean-ing of con-tent-ment,
ease;_____ There is on-ly one true an-swer,

FADED LOVE

Words and Music by BOB WILLS
and JOHNNY WILLS

Moderato

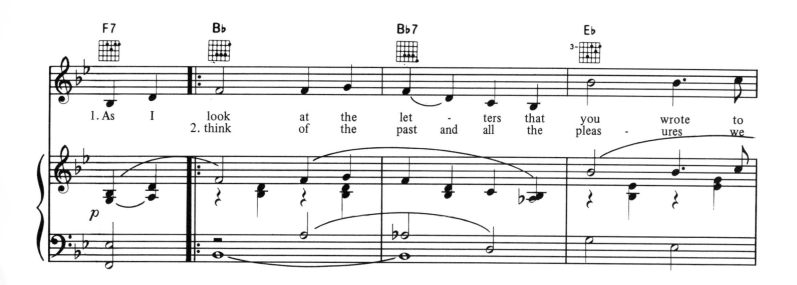

1. As I look at the let - ters that you wrote to me
2. think of the past and all the pleas - ures we had

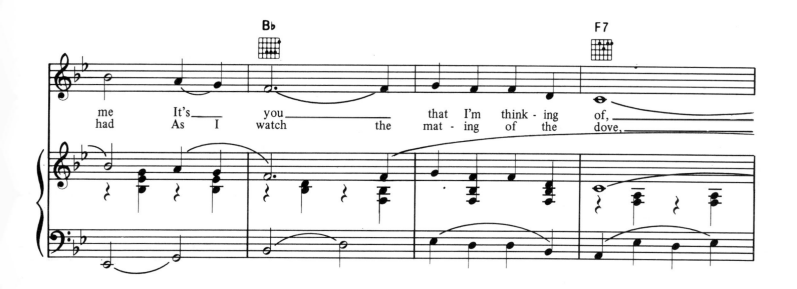

It's you that I'm think - ing of,
As I watch the mat - ing of the dove,

CRYING MY HEART OUT OVER YOU

Words and Music by CARL BUTLER, MARIJOHN WILKIN,
LOUISE CERTAIN and GLADYS STACEY

Medium Country

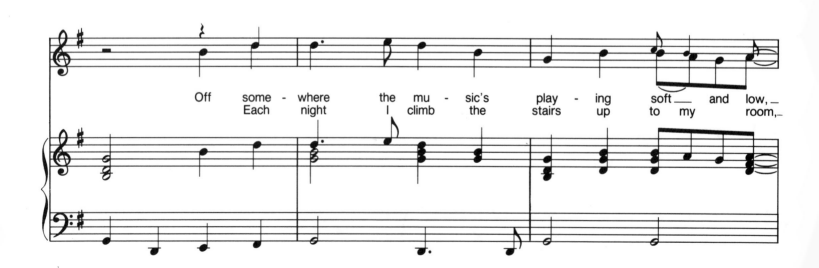

Off some - where the mu - sic's play - ing soft __ and low, __
Each night I climb the stairs up to my room, __

lit - tle more each day 'cause I'm cry - ing my

heart out o - ver you.

you.

DEEP IN THE HEART OF TEXAS

Words by JUNE HERSHEY
Music by DON SWANDER

Moderately bright

There is a land, a west - ern

land, might - y won - der - ful to

see. _____ It is the

Tex - as; _____ The prai - rie
Tex - as; _____ The rab - bits

sky is wide and high,
rush a - round and the brush,
(Clap Clap Clap

deep in the heart of Tex - as. _____
deep in the heart of Tex - as. _____
Clap)

The sage in bloom is like per -
The cow - boys cry, "Ki - yip - pee -

DON'T LET THE STARS GET IN YOUR EYES

Words and Music by
SLIM WILLET

FOR THE GOOD TIMES

Words and Music by
KRIS KRISTOFFERSON

GONE

Words and Music by
SMOKEY ROGERS

Slowly

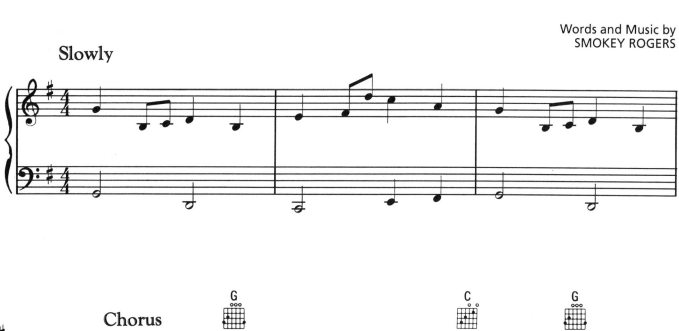

Chorus

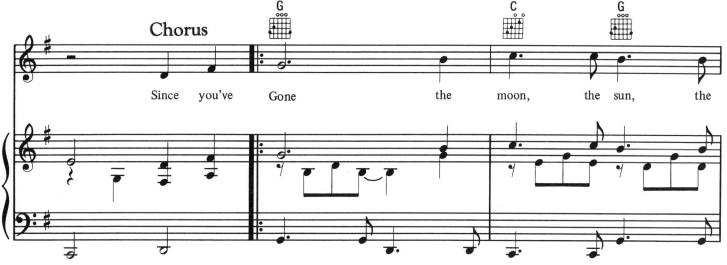

Since you've Gone the moon, the sun, the

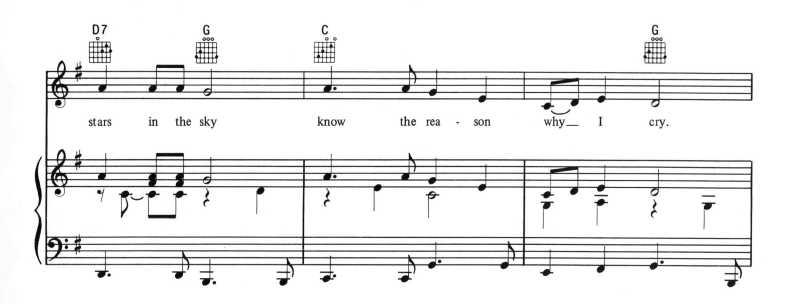

stars in the sky know the rea - son why__ I cry.

FUNNY HOW TIME SLIPS AWAY

Words and Music by
WILLIE NELSON

GREEN GREEN GRASS OF HOME

Words and Music by
CURLY PUTMAN

Moderately Slow

It's good to touch the green, green grass of home._____ The

old home town__ looks the same as I step down from the
old house is still stand - ing tho' the paint is cracked and

(Spoken:) Then I awake and look around me at four gray
walls

train,_____ and there to meet me is my ma - ma__ and
dry,_____ and there's that old oak tree that I used__ to

that surround me and I realize that I was only dreaming.

HALF AS MUCH

Words and Music by
CURLEY WILLIAMS

Moderately

If you loved me half as much as I love you, _____ you would-n't wor - ry me half as much as you do. _____ You're nice to

stay a - way half as much as you do. ____

I know that I would nev - er be this blue. ____

If you on - ly loved me half as much as I love

you. ____ If you you. ____

8vb

HAVE I TOLD YOU LATELY THAT I LOVE YOU

Words and Music by
SCOTT WISEMAN

With movement

MCA Music Publishing

HE'LL HAVE TO GO

Words and Music by JOE ALLISON
and AUDREY ALLISON

HEARTACHES BY THE NUMBER

Words and Music by
HARLAN HOWARD

HELLO WALLS

Words and Music by
WILLIE NELSON

79

ceil - ing, _____ I'm gon - na stare at you a - while you know I

can't sleep, so won't you bear with me a - while? We must

all pull to - geth - er or else I'll lose my mind, 'cause I've got a

feel - in' she'll be gone a long, long time. _____

HELP ME MAKE IT THROUGH THE NIGHT

Words and Music by
KRIS KRISTOFFERSON

Moderato

82

HEY, GOOD LOOKIN'

Words and Music by
HANK WILLIAMS

Moderately

I CAN'T HELP IT
(If I'm Still in Love with You)

Words and Music by
HANK WILLIAMS

Mournfully

I CAN'T STOP LOVING YOU

Words and Music by
DON GIBSON

I REALLY DON'T WANT TO KNOW

Words by HOWARD BARNES
Music by DON ROBERTSON

Moderately slow

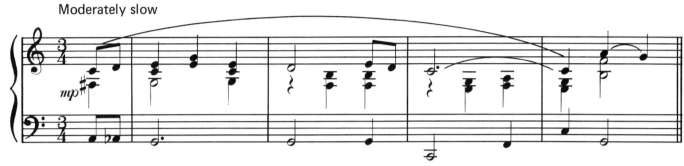

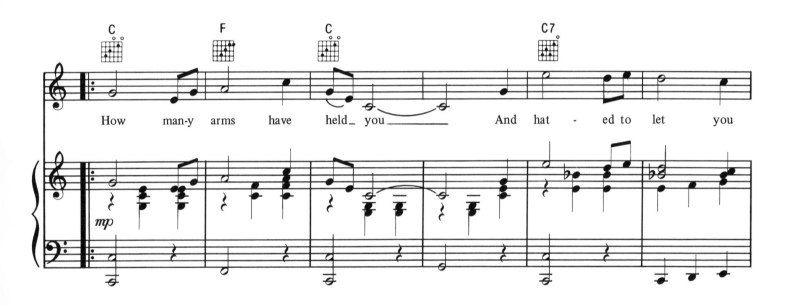

How man-y arms have held_ you _____ And hat - ed to let you

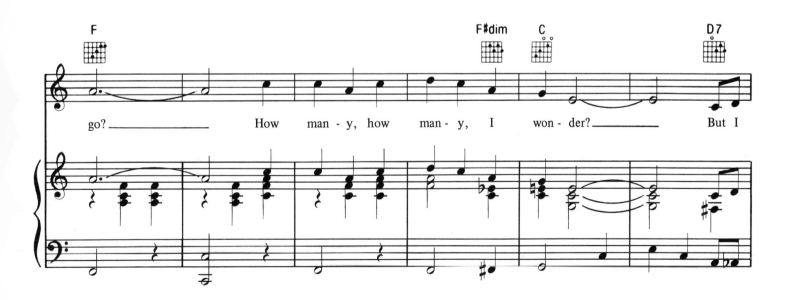

go? _____ How man - y, how man - y, I won - der? _____ But I

94

I FALL TO PIECES

Words and Music by HANK COCHRAN
and HARLAN HOWARD

Moderate Country 2

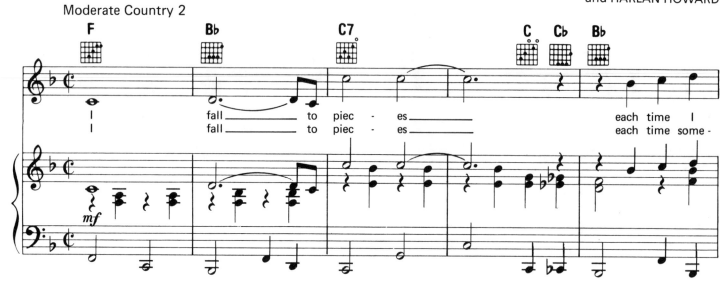

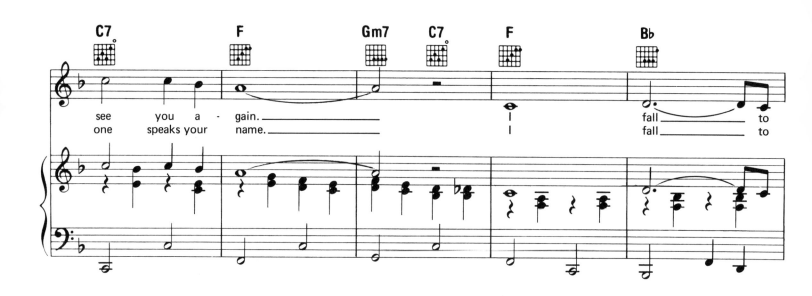

I WALK THE LINE

Words and Music by
JOHN R. CASH

Line. 2. I find it

3. - 5. *See additional lyrics*

Line.

Additional Lyrics

3. As sure as night is dark and day is light,
I keep you on my mind both day and night.
And happiness I've known proves that it's right.
Because you're mine I Walk The Line.

4. You've got a way to keep me on your side.
You give me cause for love that I can't hide.
For you I know I'd even try to turn the tide.
Because you're mine I Walk The Line.

5. I keep a close watch on this heart of mine.
I keep my eyes wide open all the time.
I keep the ends out for the tie that binds.
Because you're mine I Walk The Line.

I'M SO LONESOME I COULD CRY

Words and Music by
HANK WILLIAMS

I'M THINKING TONIGHT OF MY BLUE EYES

Words and Music by
A.P. CARTER

JAMBALAYA
(On the Bayou)

Words and Music by
HANK WILLIAMS

3. Settle down far from town, get me a pirogue
   And I'll catch all the fish in the bayou
   Swap my mon to buy Yvonne what whe need-o
   Son of a gun, we'll have big fun on the bayou

JEALOUS HEART

Words and Music by
JENNY LOU CARSON

JUST A LITTLE LOVIN'
(Will Go a Long Way)

Words and Music by ZEKE CLEMENTS
and EDDY ARNOLD

THE LAST WORD IN LONESOME IS ME

Words and Music by
ROGER MILLER

MAKE THE WORLD GO AWAY

Words and Music by
HANK COCHRAN

MY HEART CRIES FOR YOU

Music by PERCY FAITH
Lyrics by CARL SIGMAN

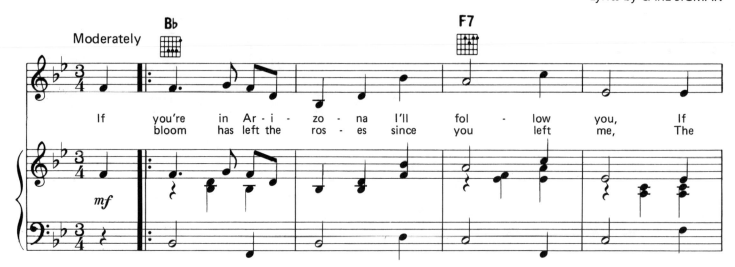

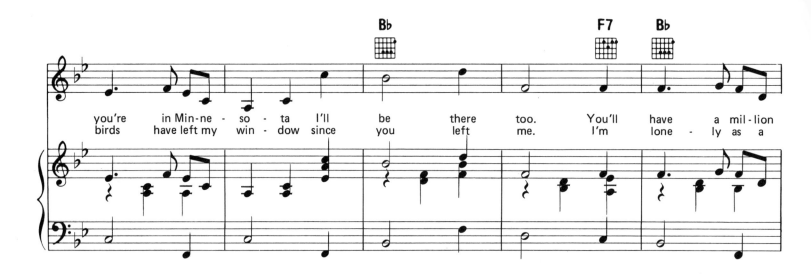

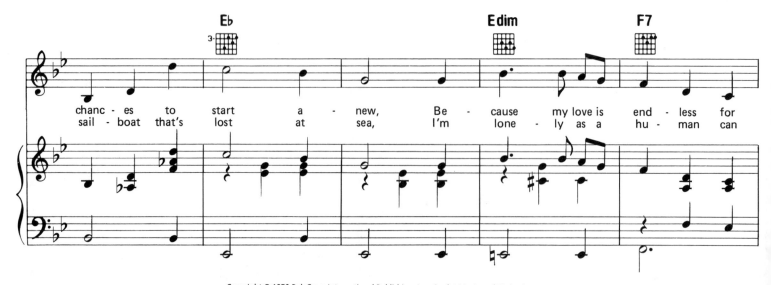

MY SHOES KEEP WALKING BACK TO YOU

Words and Music by LEE ROSS
and BOB WILLS

Slowly, with expression

I must say that I don't care Hold my head up in the air E-ven tell my friends I'm
how much I pre-tend I wish I had you back a-gain For noth-in' else means

glad that you don't call_____ But_____ when the day is thru My
half as much as you_____ Our_____ world just seemed to die The

heart-ache starts a-new And that's when I miss you most of all:_____
day you said good-bye And I can't for-get no mat-ter what I do:_____

OH, LONESOME ME

Words and Music by
DON GIBSON

123

arms_____ Well, there must be some way I can lose these lone-some blues_____

__ For - get a - bout the past and find some - bod - y new_____ I've

thought of ev - 'ry - thing from A to Z_____ oh,_____

__ lone - some me._____

ROOM FULL OF ROSES

Words and Music by
TIM SPENCER

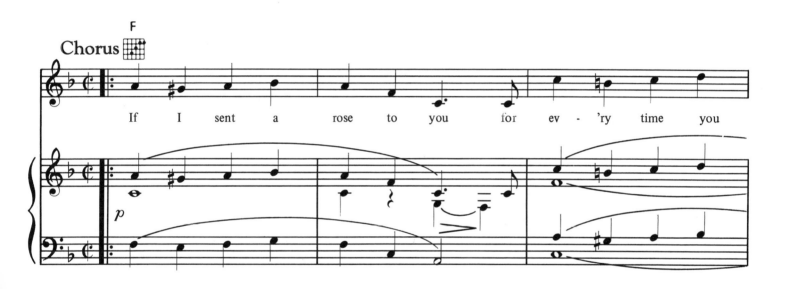

If I sent a rose to you for ev - 'ry time you

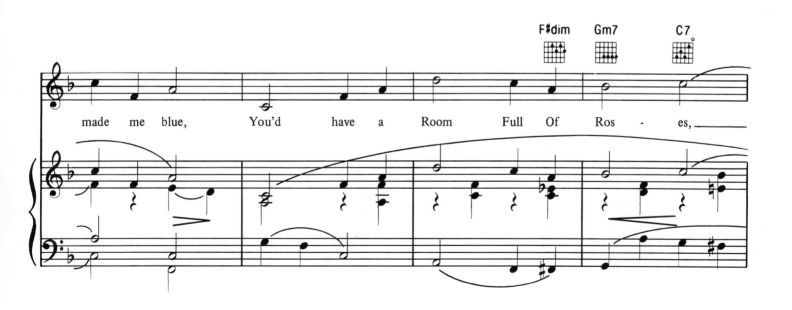

made me blue, You'd have a Room Full Of Ros - es,

PAPER ROSES

Words by JANICE TORRE
Music by FRED SPIELMAN

SEND ME THE PILLOW YOU DREAM ON

Words and Music by
HANK LOCKLIN

SINGING THE BLUES

Words and Music by
MELVIN ENDSLEY

TENNESSEE WALTZ

Words and Music by REDD STEWART
and PEE WEE KING

SIXTEEN TONS

Words and Music by
MERLE TRAVIS

SWEET DREAMS

Words and Music by
DON GIBSON

WALKIN' AFTER MIDNIGHT

Lyrics by DON HECHT
Music by ALAN W. BLOCK

WALKING THE FLOOR OVER YOU

Words and Music by
ERNEST TUBB

Swingy tempo

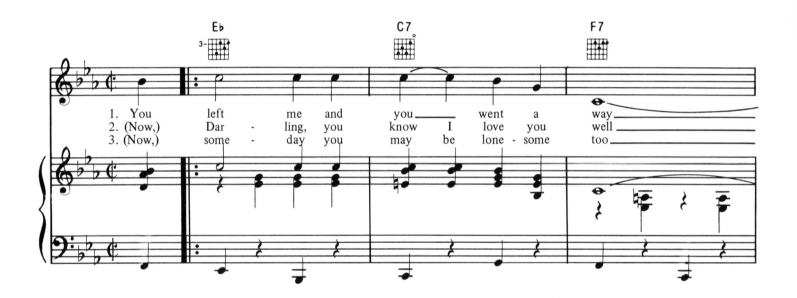

1. You left me and you_____ went a way_____
2. (Now,) Dar - ling, you know I love you well_____
3. (Now,) some - day you may be lone - some too_____

You said that you'd be back in just a day_____
Love you more than I can ev - er tell_____
Walk - ing the floor is good for you_____

WELCOME TO MY WORLD

Words and Music by RAY WINKLER
and JOHN HATHCOCK

WHEN MY BLUE MOON TURNS TO GOLD AGAIN

Words and Music by WILEY WALKER
and GENE SULLIVAN

With movement

YOU ARE MY SUNSHINE

Words and Music by JIMMIE DAVIS
and CHARLES MITCHELL

154

YOU DON'T KNOW ME

Words and Music by CINDY WALKER
and EDDY ARNOLD

156

YOUR CHEATIN' HEART

Words and Music by
HANK WILLIAMS

160